FREEDOM'S
PROMISE

THE TULSA
RACE RIOT

BY DUCHESS HARRIS, JD, PHD
WITH A. R. CARSER

Core Library

An Imprint of Abdo Publishing
abdobooks.com

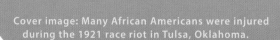

Cover image: Many African Americans were injured
during the 1921 race riot in Tulsa, Oklahoma.

abdocorelibrary.com

Published by Abdo Publishing, a division of ABDO, PO Box 398166, Minneapolis, Minnesota 55439. Copyright © 2020 by Abdo Consulting Group, Inc. International copyrights reserved in all countries. No part of this book may be reproduced in any form without written permission from the publisher. Core Library™ is a trademark and logo of Abdo Publishing.

Printed in the United States of America, North Mankato, Minnesota
032019
092019

THIS BOOK CONTAINS
RECYCLED MATERIALS

Cover Photo: American National Red Cross Photograph Collection/Library of Congress
Interior Photos: American National Red Cross Photograph Collection/Library of Congress, 1, 5, 26–27, 29; Everett Collection/Newscom, 6–7, 34–35; Everett Historical/Shutterstock Images, 11; MPI/Archive Photos/Getty Images, 13; Corbis/Corbis Historical/Getty Images, 16–17, 43; Red Line Editorial, 24, 31; Oklahoma Historical Society/Archive Photos/Getty Images, 22–23; Gerald Herbert/AP Images, 39

Editor: Maddie Spalding
Series Designer: Claire Vanden Branden

Library of Congress Control Number: 2018966000

Publisher's Cataloging-in-Publication Data

Names: Harris, Duchess, author | Carser, A. R., author.
Title: The Tulsa race riot / by Duchess Harris and A. R. Carser
Description: Minneapolis, Minnesota: Abdo Publishing, 2020 | Series: Freedom's promise | Includes online resources and index.
Identifiers: ISBN 9781532118807 (lib. bdg.) | ISBN 9781532172984 (ebook)
Subjects: LCSH: Race riots--Juvenile literature. | Southern States--Race relations--History--20th century--Juvenile literature. | African Americans--Social conditions--Juvenile literature. | Violence--United States--History--Juvenile literature.
Classification: DDC 305.800973--dc23

CONTENTS

A LETTER FROM DUCHESS

In this book, you will learn about Black Wall Street. Wall Street is the nation's financial district in New York City. Black Wall Street was a nickname for the neighborhood of Greenwood in Tulsa, Oklahoma, in the early 1900s. Black people established many successful businesses there.

African Americans began migrating to Oklahoma in the late 1800s. Oklahoma offered the promise of a better life for many formerly enslaved Black people. A thriving Black middle class settled in Greenwood. As the Black community flourished, hatred did as well. With veterans returning from World War I and jobs becoming scarcer, envy and racial tension grew among some white Tulsans. As a result, angry white people burned down the prosperous African American neighborhood in 1921. They destroyed Black Wall Street and killed many African Americans.

Please join me in remembering the victims of the Tulsa race riot. This story is a reminder of the often-deadly challenges African Americans faced as they reached for the American dream.

Duchess Harris

Greenwood residents had to build new homes after the Tulsa race riot.

CHAPTER
ONE

IS THE WORLD ON FIRE?

I t was daybreak on June 1, 1921. Five-year-old George Monroe heard men's voices on his porch. He peeked out the front door. The men were white. They carried torches. George and his four siblings were alone. Their parents had left for work. Frightened, they hid under a bed.

The men were targeting George and his family because they were African American. They broke into George's home. They used their torches to set the curtains on fire.

The men left. But now George's home was on fire. He and his siblings ran outside

A mob of white people burned hundreds of buildings in Greenwood on June 1, 1921.

MOUNT ZION BAPTIST CHURCH

In the early 1900s, black people were segregated in public places. Black and white people did not go to the same churches. Black churches were important spaces within African American communities. They were spaces where black people could gather and support one another through difficult times. Greenwood's Mount Zion Baptist Church opened in April 1921. Community members had spent years raising money to build the brick church. The beautiful structure was a place to worship. It was also a symbol of Greenwood's wealth. White people burned it to the ground during the Tulsa riot. It took the community many years to rebuild the church.

to safety. Other homes on their block were also on fire. They ran to Mount Zion Baptist Church nearby. But the brick church was also burning. Angry white people had looted and burned George's entire neighborhood. George turned to his older sister. Terrified, he asked, "Is the world on fire?"

BLACK WALL STREET

George and his family lived in Greenwood. Greenwood is a neighborhood in

Tulsa, Oklahoma. It was home to Tulsa's successful African American community. Some of the community's residents owned hotels, restaurants, and stores. Others were lawyers or teachers. Many were maids, drivers, or gardeners for wealthy white people. The community's average wage was among the highest for African Americans in the South. The success of many black businesspeople in Greenwood had earned the neighborhood the nickname "Black Wall Street." Wall Street is a street in New York City where many financial companies do business.

Housing rules separated white and black residents in Tulsa. On a block where at least three-fourths of people were one race, it was illegal for a person of another race to live there. This law kept black people from living in white communities. Black and white children could not attend the same schools. Black Tulsans lived in Greenwood. White Tulsans lived everywhere else in the city. Tulsa's laws were similar to many other laws across the South. These rules, called Jim Crow Laws, enforced racial segregation.

TROUBLE BREWING

In 1905 oil was discovered near Tulsa. Americans across the country moved to the city. White men worked in the oil fields. But African American men were not allowed to hold these jobs. Instead they opened businesses that fed, housed, and entertained the oil workers. Tulsa grew rapidly.

The oil boom created wealth for Tulsa's black and white residents. Both populations grew quickly. Racism was everywhere in Tulsa. The city's newspapers made racist remarks. Ministers in some of the city's white churches spread racist beliefs.

Meanwhile Greenwood continued to grow. Black-owned businesses in the community became successful. Some black business owners spoke out against racist laws. Their success and defense of their rights frightened many white Tulsans. These white

In the early 1900s, black students had to attend separate schools from white students.

residents believed that African Americans made Tulsa unsafe and dirty. They thought their black neighbors were criminals. This was not true. But the state's Jim Crow laws reinforced these racist ideas.

MOB VIOLENCE

In the early 1900s, mob violence was common in the United States. Mob attacks and murders of African Americans rose sharply between 1917 and 1919. Murders committed by mobs are called lynchings. A white terrorist group called the Ku Klux Klan committed many lynchings.

The National Association for the Advancement of Colored People (NAACP) took immediate action. The NAACP is a group that protects African Americans' civil rights. In 1917 it began an antilynching campaign. It organized protests against lynching.

The NAACP organized nonviolent protests and marches against lynching in the early 1900s.

In September 1919, an article in the NAACP's *Crisis* magazine urged black people to defend themselves against mob violence and racism. In Tulsa, a black newspaper called the *Tulsa Star* also offered advice. It urged black Tulsans not to respond violently to racist behavior. Any violence or perceived violence could be used as an excuse to lynch black people.

A LYNCHING IN TULSA

On August 21, 1920, a white taxi driver named Homer Nida picked up three white passengers in Tulsa. One of the passengers shot Nida. The passengers left Nida to die on the side of the road. Nida survived long enough to describe the passengers to the police. He identified his attacker as 18-year-old Roy Belton. Belton confessed to the attack. Nida later died, and Belton was arrested and charged with murder.

On the evening of August 28, a mob of approximately 1,000 people gathered outside the courthouse where Belton was being held. The sheriff was inside the courthouse. Approximately 50 men in the mob were armed. They broke into the courthouse. They disarmed the sheriff. The men captured Belton. They led him outside to the waiting mob.

The armed men drove Belton outside of town in Nida's taxi cab. Most of the mob followed. The Tulsa police also followed the men. But the police chief told his officers that they should not try to stop the lynching. The mob hanged Belton.

Reporters at the *Tulsa World* praised the lynching. Tulsa's police chief said that the lynching could not have been avoided. In Greenwood, the lynching created doubts and fear. Tulsa police had not protected a white prisoner from mob violence. Many Greenwood residents thought it even less likely that police would protect black prisoners from mob violence.

EXPLORE ONLINE

Chapter One talks about black-owned newspapers in the early 1900s and how they responded to violence. Newspapers were segregated at that time. The website below goes into more depth on the history of black newspapers. How is the information from the website the same as the information in Chapter One? What new information did you learn from the website?

SOLDIERS WITHOUT SWORDS
abdocorelibrary.com/tulsa-race-riot

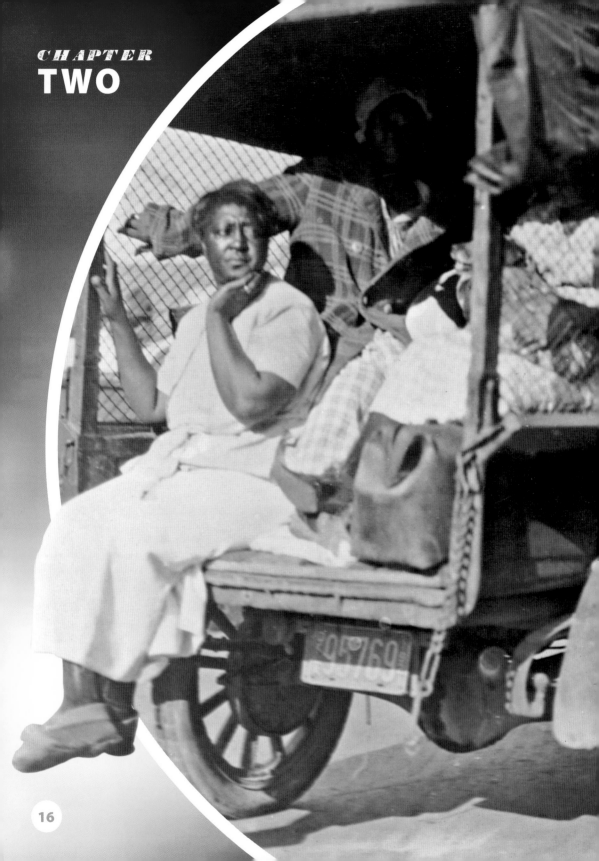

TULSA BURNING

On May 30, 1921, African American shoe shiner Dick Rowland needed to use the bathroom. He took the elevator in Tulsa's Drexel Building up to the top floor. That is where the blacks-only bathroom was.

What exactly happened in the elevator is still unknown. Most historians believe Rowland tripped. To catch his fall, he reached for the arm of the white elevator operator. Her name was Sarah Page. She cried out. Another person in the building heard her. He called the police. He told the police that he thought Rowland had sexually assaulted Page. At first the police were not convinced. But rumors of an attack

Many Greenwood residents fled the neighborhood for their safety during the Tulsa race riot.

quickly spread. In the face of mounting pressure, the police decided to arrest Rowland.

On May 31, the *Tulsa Tribune* reported on Rowland's arrest. The *Tribune* was a white newspaper. It claimed that Rowland had attacked Page in the elevator. The paper encouraged violence against Rowland. About one hour after the paper was published, white Tulsans gathered on the steps of the Tulsa County Courthouse. They were united in one goal: to lynch Rowland. Rowland was being held on the top floor of the building.

By evening the mob had grown to hundreds of people. Sheriff Willard M.

ROWLAND'S FATE

During the riot, Dick Rowland may have been the safest person in Tulsa. While violence raged in Greenwood, the sheriff and his officers continued to guard Rowland. On the day of the riot, police questioned Sarah Page. She refused to press charges against Rowland. On June 1, armed guards moved Rowland out of town for his safety. Rowland never returned to Tulsa.

McCullough was on alert. He ordered armed deputies to protect Rowland. He stationed more deputies on the courthouse roof. McCullough urged the mob to go home. Instead they shouted insults at him.

GREENWOOD REACTS

Greenwood residents soon learned about the mob at the courthouse. They met to decide how to keep Rowland safe. The Belton lynching was fresh on their minds. Most people did not think law enforcement would be willing or able to protect Rowland. The mob was angry, and it was growing.

At about 7:30 p.m., a group of 30 black men made their way to the courthouse. They carried guns. They offered to help McCullough defend Rowland. But the sheriff turned them away.

By late evening, the white mob had grown to nearly 2,000 people. Meanwhile small groups of armed Greenwood residents drove to the courthouse. They wanted to know what was happening there.

Many people in the mob thought that Tulsa's black residents were invading white Tulsa.

At about 10:00 p.m., one more group of armed black men went to the courthouse. They offered their support to the sheriff. He turned them away. Several people in the mob confronted the men. One white man asked a black man to turn over his pistol. The black man refused. A shot was fired. No one knew who fired the shot or whether it had been fired on purpose. The shot did not hit anyone. But it immediately led to a shoot-out.

THE VIOLENCE CONTINUES

Within a few minutes, ten white people and two black people had been killed. The black men tried to return to Greenwood. But the white mob chased after them. Fighting continued along the train tracks near Greenwood.

At about 1:00 a.m., groups of white people broke into black-owned businesses in Greenwood. They stole goods from stores and set buildings on fire. The Tulsa Fire Department tried to put out the fires. But the mob turned firefighters away at gunpoint. The mob continued to burn buildings throughout the night.

By daybreak on June 1, many Greenwood residents had fled the neighborhood. Others stayed behind to protect their property. As the sun rose, the violence increased.

PERSPECTIVES
J. B. STRADFORD

J. B. Stradford owned the Stradford Hotel in Greenwood. During the Tulsa race riot, Stradford stood in the doorway of his hotel to defend it against attackers. The Oklahoma National Guard persuaded him to leave his hotel for his own safety. Guardsmen assured him that his hotel would not be touched. But rioters burned the Stradford Hotel to the ground. Police charged Stradford with inciting the riot. But Stradford had gone to the courthouse to try to stop violence from breaking out. Stradford's great-grandson, Cornelius E. Toole, later helped clear Stradford's name. Toole said, "He had the same dreams as all Americans, and a race riot stopped it."

Black Wall Street was in ruins after the Tulsa race riot.

Armed white Tulsans poured into Greenwood. They broke into homes and businesses. They burned buildings to the ground.

At 11:49 a.m., the Oklahoma National Guard declared martial law. Martial law puts the military in charge of a government. The National Guard took over

the governance of Tulsa. The purpose of martial law

is to maintain public order and safety. White people

had committed most of the violence. But the guards

rounded up African Americans. The guards marched

them at gunpoint to vacant buildings throughout

the city. The guards confined African Americans in

these spaces.

TIMELINE OF THE RIOT

May 31, 1921

3:00 p.m.
The *Tulsa Tribune* claims that Dick Rowland assaulted Sarah Page.

4:00 p.m.
A mob of white people gather at the Tulsa courthouse where Rowland is being held.

10:00 p.m.
The mob grows to 2,000 people. A group of Greenwood residents arrives at the courthouse.

10:30 p.m.
The mob and Greenwood residents argue. A shot is fired. A shoot-out follows.

June 1, 1921

12:00–1:30 a.m.
The white mob begins to loot and set fire to buildings in Greenwood.

9:15 a.m.
The Oklahoma National Guard arrives in Tulsa.

11:49 a.m.
The National Guard declares martial law in Tulsa. Guardsmen round up black Tulsans.

The above timeline shows the events that happened before and during the riot. How does this timeline help you better understand these events and how they are connected?

THE AFTERMATH

The fires devastated Greenwood. Entire blocks were destroyed. The white mob had burned down 191 businesses and 1,256 homes.

The exact number of people killed in the attack is unknown. The attack was called a race riot. A race riot is a sudden outbreak of violence motivated by racial hatred. The *Tulsa Tribune* initially reported that 176 people died in the riot. The day after this report was published, the newspaper came out with a different number. It said that 30 people had died. The *New York Times* initially reported a similar number. It said that 33 people died. The American Red Cross came to the scene shortly after the violence to aid victims. The Red Cross surveyed the damage. It recorded that approximately 300 people died. Most historians today believe the Red Cross's estimate is most accurate.

FURTHER EVIDENCE

Chapter Two covers the events of the Tulsa race riot. What was one of the main points of this chapter? What evidence is included to support this point? Read the article at the website below. Does the information on the website support this point? Does it present new evidence?

1921 TULSA RACE RIOT
abdocorelibrary.com/tulsa-race-riot

CHAPTER THREE

RISING FROM THE ASHES

Martial law in Tulsa lasted two days. By June 2, the National Guard had moved all black Tulsans to the state fairgrounds. Armed guards forced more than 4,000 people into animal pens. They gave the people some food, clothing, and bedding. But they did not give wounded people medical care. In the first few days, the guards only allowed a few people to leave. The guards finally released everyone in mid-June.

White Tulsans used the riot as an excuse to mistreat black Tulsans. They created a new system to control African Americans. Black Tulsans were required to carry cards

It took Greenwood residents years to rebuild their neighborhood after the Tulsa race riot.

PLANES OVER GREENWOOD

After the riot, many victims reported that airplanes had attacked Greenwood. They remembered seeing people shooting from the airplanes. Some saw planes dropping bombs on the neighborhood. But law enforcement said that this did not happen. Law enforcement did fly planes over the neighborhood. But they claimed that they did not use these planes to attack people. They said that they were just keeping an eye on Greenwood residents. The available evidence supports this. Many other survivors' accounts do not mention plane attacks. The film and video footage does not show a plane attack. For these reasons, many historians believe that the planes did not attack Greenwood.

with their names and addresses. Law enforcement regularly stopped black people and asked them to show their cards. Officers arrested anyone who could not produce this card. This system lasted until early July.

HELPING VICTIMS

In the days after the riot, the Red Cross created an emergency hospital. Red Cross workers offered first aid. They helped people find jobs. Many Greenwood

The American Red Cross aided survivors of the Tulsa race riot.

residents became unemployed after their businesses or workplaces were burned to the ground. The Red Cross also gave people clothing and groceries. It provided tents for families to use as temporary housing.

The East End Welfare Board also supported victims of the riot. Greenwood residents formed this group to help their neighbors. The East End Welfare Board worked with the Red Cross. The NAACP also raised money for riot victims.

BROKEN PROMISES

The Oklahoma state government did not give much aid to the victims. The National Guard refused to provide tents to the Red Cross. Other cities offered to give aid to Tulsans. But government officials turned down their offers.

After the riot, the Tulsa Chamber of Commerce created the Executive Welfare Committee. This committee called the riot shameful. It said the riot was a disgrace on the city. It promised to pay victims for their losses. But the committee did not fulfill this promise. It did not collect donations from people who wanted to help Greenwood recover. Instead it made a plan for white business owners to purchase property from black people. The fires had greatly reduced the price of the land. If white business owners bought the land, black families could not rebuild their community. White business owners wanted to create a business district in Tulsa. But this plan was never carried out.

Two weeks after the riot, the mayor of Tulsa created the Reconstruction Committee. This committee took the place of the Executive Welfare Committee. It did even

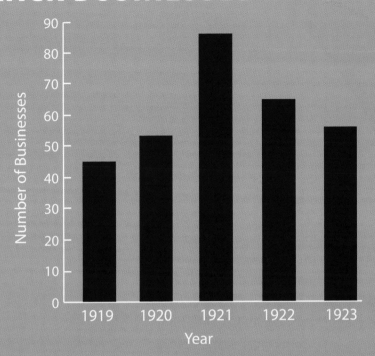

BLACK BUSINESSES IN TULSA

The Tulsa race riot had a significant effect on the number of black businesses in Tulsa. The above graph shows how many of these businesses existed before and after the riot. How does this graph help you better understand the riot's damage?

less to raise funds to rebuild Greenwood. By the end of the summer, the committee had disbanded.

Greenwood residents rebuilt their neighborhood after the attack. This process was difficult. Insurance companies would not pay for damages caused by a riot. Residents had to pay for the damages themselves.

A GRAND JURY

On June 2, 1921, the city of Tulsa put together a grand jury. A grand jury is a group of people that reviews evidence. It decides whether a crime has occurred. The jury's purpose was to investigate who was responsible for the Tulsa race riot. The jury included only white people. It blamed black people for the riot. Law enforcement did not arrest any white people.

STRAIGHT TO THE
SOURCE

Some historians say the attack on Greenwood should be called a massacre, not a race riot. A riot is violence committed by a group that wants to cause disruption. A massacre is the killing of helpless people out of cruelty. The Tulsa Historical Society says,

> In recent years there has been ongoing discussion about what to call the event that happened in 1921. Historically, it has been called the Tulsa Race Riot. Some say it was given that name at the time for insurance purposes. Designating it a riot prevented insurance companies from having to pay benefits to the people of Greenwood whose homes and businesses were destroyed. It also was common at the time for any large-scale clash between different racial or ethnic groups to be categorized a race riot.

> Source: "1921 Tulsa Race Riot." *Tulsa Historical Society & Museum*. Tulsa Historical Society & Museum, n.d. Web. Accessed September 12, 2018.

Point of View

The Tulsa Historical Society explains why people at the time called the attack on Greenwood a race riot. Do you think the incident should be called a riot or a massacre? Why? Use evidence from this book to support your opinion.

THE RIOT'S LEGACY

On June 1, 1971, the *Tulsa Tribune* published a story about the Tulsa race riot. It was the first major story about the riot to appear in the city's newspapers since 1921. The reporter who wrote the story did not blame anyone for the attacks. But this was an important step in acknowledging that the event had happened. Still, the *Tribune* did not acknowledge that it had played a role in encouraging mob violence.

Many white people in Oklahoma and around the country tried to bury or ignore the story of the Tulsa race riot. The attack was not included in any local or state history books.

A truck picked up injured people during the Tulsa race riot.

DON ROSS

Don Ross is an African American writer. He grew up in Greenwood in the 1950s. A black teacher taught him about the Tulsa race riot when he was in high school. Ross later created a magazine called *Impact*. In 1971 he published an article he had written about the riot in his magazine. Ross became an Oklahoma state lawmaker in 1982. He advocated for the creation of a commission to study the Tulsa race riot. He plans to write a book about Tulsa's African American history. He says, "I want to write about how segregation molded the community, and the different laws and changes that have been made."

Most students in Oklahoma did not learn about the riot in school until 2012. In that year, the Oklahoma House of Representatives passed a law. The law required educators to teach their students about the riot.

REPARATIONS

In 2001 the Oklahoma government created the Oklahoma Commission to Study the Tulsa Race Riot of 1921. This commission reviewed the cause of the event. It assessed the riot's damage.

It used this information to make a case for who was responsible.

The commission estimated that 100 to 300 people were killed during the riot. The commission recommended that the state pay reparations to the victims of the riot. Reparations are payments or help offered to victims or their families as an apology. Oklahoma lawmakers accepted the findings of the report. On behalf of white Tulsans, the Oklahoma State Legislature accepted the responsibility for the riot. But the legislature refused to pay any reparations to the families of riot victims.

Since 2001 more than 200 people have sued the state for reparations. Most have asked for scholarships or medical support. But courts have denied these requests. In Oklahoma, people who have had their civil rights violated have just two years to sue for damages. After two years, they can no longer file a lawsuit. In 2007 a group tried to change this. The Reparations

Coordinating Committee introduced a law to US Congress. It was called the John Hope Franklin Tulsa-Greenwood Race Riot Claims Accountability Act. It would allow victims of the riot and their families to seek reparations. The proposed law has been discussed in Congress every year since 2007. But the act has yet to become law.

NEW DISCOVERIES

In 1998 archaeologists made a discovery in Tulsa. They believed they had found three mass grave sites. Victims of the Tulsa race riot could be buried in these sites. The sites are large enough to hold hundreds of bodies. The city refused to allow the archaeologists to study the sites. The mayor said it would be too costly. It would also disturb other graves near the sites. But in 2018, Tulsa's mayor gave permission for an investigation. Studying the sites could provide more information about the riot. It could give people a better idea of how many people died during the riot.

GREENWOOD TODAY

Today many thriving businesses line Greenwood Avenue. Some have plaques describing the businesses that

Otis Clarke, *right*, a survivor of the Tulsa race riot, sought reparations from the US government in 2005.

existed there before the riot. People in Greenwood

and Tulsa have made efforts to teach people about the

riot. The John Hope Franklin Reconciliation Park has a

memorial to the victims and survivors. The Greenwood Cultural Center teaches visitors about the riot and the neighborhood's history. The Tulsa Historical Society and Museum has an exhibit about the riot. It includes recordings of survivors sharing their memories of the attack. The historical society has made these stories available to the public for free. Greenwood residents and historians hope Americans will learn and pass along the story of the Tulsa race riot.

STRAIGHT TO THE
SOURCE

The Oklahoma Commission to Study the Tulsa Race Riot of 1921 had a difficult job. No other group had attempted to thoroughly investigate the event. In its report, the commission wrote:

> [The riot] happened. There was murder, false imprisonment, forced labor, a cover-up. . . . While the official damage was estimated at $1.5 million, the black community filed more than $4 million in claims. All were denied. . . . The issue today is what government entity should provide financial repair to the survivors and the condemned community that suffered under vigilante violence? The Report tells the story, let justice point the finger and begin the reconciliation!

> Source: "Tulsa Race Riot: A Report by the Oklahoma Commission to Study the Tulsa Race Riot of 1921." *Oklahoma Historical Society*. Oklahoma Historical Society, February 28, 2001. Web. Accessed September 12, 2018. viii.

Consider Your Audience

Adapt this passage for a different audience, such as your friends. Write a blog post conveying this same information for the new audience. How does your post differ from the original text and why?

FAST FACTS

- In the early 1900s, cities throughout the South were racially segregated. This included the city of Tulsa, Oklahoma. Most of Tulsa's black residents lived in a neighborhood called Greenwood.

- On May 30, 1921, a black man was accused of assaulting a white woman. The next day, police arrested the man. An angry white mob wanted to lynch the man. They gathered outside the courthouse. Greenwood residents came to the scene. Violence erupted, and the white mob began attacking Greenwood. The mob burned more than 1,000 buildings and killed approximately 300 people.

- Most people blamed African Americans for the riot. The Oklahoma National Guard came to Tulsa. Guardsmen gathered up thousands of African Americans and put them in animal pens for several days.

- After the riot, Greenwood residents rebuilt their community with little help from white Tulsans.

- In 2001 the Commission to Study the Tulsa Race Riot of 1921 found that the Oklahoma state government had the responsibility to pay reparations to the victims of the attack.

- Today several organizations in Greenwood are devoted to telling the story of the Tulsa race riot.

STOP AND
THINK

Tell the Tale

Chapter One describes one person's experience during the Tulsa race riot. Imagine you are returning to Greenwood after the riot. Write 200 words about what you see. How was the neighborhood damaged after the riot?

Take a Stand

Chapter Five discusses reparations for the victims of the Tulsa race riot and their families. Do you think the state of Oklahoma has a responsibility to pay survivors and their families for the damages they suffered from the riot? Why or why not?

Why Do I Care?

The Tulsa race riot happened about 100 years ago. But that doesn't mean you can't think about how it continues to affect African Americans in Tulsa today. In what ways is the Greenwood community still trying to recover from the riot?

GLOSSARY

civil rights
the rights every person has
under the law

commission
an official group of people
that is asked to perform a
specific duty

grand jury
a group of people
that reviews evidence
and decides if a crime
has occurred

lawsuit
a case that is brought against
a person or group in a court

memorial
something that is created
to remember an event or
a person

racism
discrimination against
a group of people based
on their race

reparation
payment or help offered to
victims or their families as
an apology

segregation
the separation of people
of different races or
ethnic groups through
separate schools and other
public spaces

sue
to file a lawsuit

ONLINE
RESOURCES

To learn more about the Tulsa race riot, visit our free resource websites below.

Visit **abdocorelibrary.com** or scan this QR code for free Common Core resources for teachers and students, including vetted activities, multimedia, and booklinks, for deeper subject comprehension.

Visit **abdobooklinks.com** or scan this QR code for free additional online weblinks for further learning. These links are routinely monitored and updated to provide the most current information available.

LEARN
MORE

Muldoon, Kathleen M. *The Jim Crow Era*. Minneapolis, MN: Abdo Publishing, 2014.

Winter, Max. *The Civil Rights Movement*. Minneapolis, MN: Abdo Publishing, 2014.

ABOUT THE
AUTHORS

Duchess Harris, JD, PhD

Dr. Harris is a professor of American Studies at Macalester College and curator of the Duchess Harris Collection of ABDO books. She is also the coauthor of the titles in the collection, which features popular selections such as *Hidden Human Computers: The Black Women of NASA* and series including News Literacy and Being Female in America.

Before working with ABDO, Dr. Harris authored several other books on the topics of race, culture, and American history. She served as an associate editor for *Litigation News*, the American Bar Association Section of Litigation's quarterly flagship publication, and was the first editor in chief of *Law Raza*, an interactive online journal covering race and the law, published at William Mitchell College of Law. She has earned a PhD in American Studies from the University of Minnesota and a JD from William Mitchell College of Law.

A. R. Carser

A. R. Carser is a freelance writer who lives in Minnesota. She enjoys learning and writing about US history, culture, and society.

INDEX